Penny Brown
Joi Washington

HOW THE TIGER
TAKES CARE OF
HER BABIES

2 This is a tiger.

The mother tiger can have two or three cubs.

Cubs are born in a safe place like a cave or tall grass.

Many times, the cubs are born at night when it's quiet.

When the cubs are born, they can't see or hear for up to two weeks.

The mother tiger gives them milk to drink.

She has to eat more food so she can make milk for the cubs.

The mother tiger has to leave her cubs to hunt.

She hides her cubs so they will be safe while she is gone.

The cubs grow. They still drink milk. Now they eat meat, too. The mother tiger brings them lots of meat to eat.

The cubs need to know how to get meat.

The cubs learn to hunt when they play.
They jump. They run. They sneak.
This is how they learn to hunt.

Soon, the cubs go with their mother when she hunts. They watch and learn.

15

When they are two years old, the cubs
can hunt small animals on their own.

They don't need their mother
to get them food.

The cubs leave their mother when they are two years old.

They each go off and live on their own.

When the cubs are four years old, they will have their own babies.

Questions

What do tiger cubs drink when they are born?

Tigers like to eat _____.
   A) meat   B) carrots   C) trees

A tiger can't see or _____ when it's born.
   A) drink   B) hear   C) sleep

Answers

1. Milk 2. A 3. B

21

THE TIGER'S LIFE CYCLE

Adult
4-5 years

Gives birth
to cubs

Cub
1 year

Cub
Baby

Cub
3 months

USE WORDS YOU KNOW TO READ NEW WORDS!

eat
eats
seat
meat

fun
sun
hunt
hunts

or
for
corn
born

ride
rides
hide
hides

will
fill
kill
still

all
ball
mall
small

TRICKY WORDS

night   their

old   own

know   each

more